my first
jewelry making
book

my first jewelry making book

35 easy and fun projects for children aged 7 years +

CICO kidz

Published in 2013 by CICO Kidz
An imprint of Ryland Peters & Small
519 Broadway, 5th Floor, New York NY 10012
20–21 Jockey's Fields, London WC1R 4BW
www.cicobooks.com

10 9 8 7 6 5 4 3 2 1

A CIP catalog record for this book is available from
the Library of Congress and the British Library.

ISBN: 978-1-908862-71-6

Printed in China

Series consultant: Susan Akass
Editors: Susan Akass and Clare Sayer
Designers: No Days Off and Barbara Zuñiga
Step artworks: Rachel Boulton
Animal artworks: Hannah George
For photography credits, see page 127.

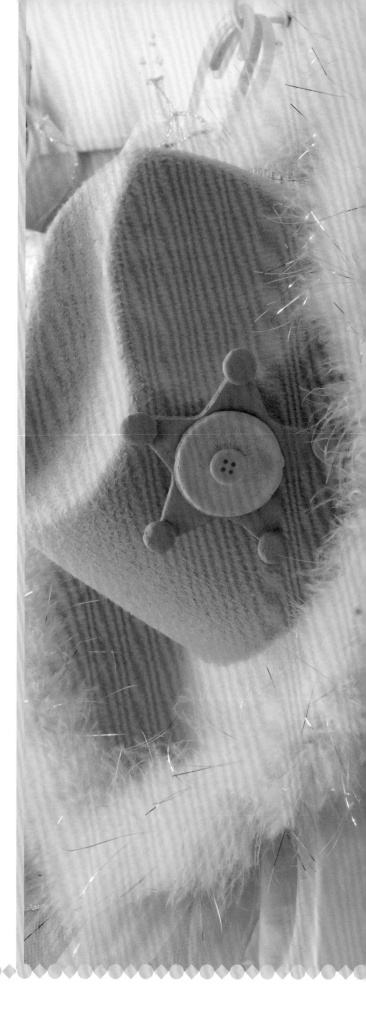

Contents

Introduction 6

CHAPTER 1
NECKLACES AND PENDANTS 8
Felt and wooden bead necklace 10
Salt dough beads 12
Felt bead necklace 16
Seed necklace 19
Rainbow felted necklace 22
Shell pendant 24
Raffia and bead necklace 26
Colorful clay pendant 28
Fabric-wrapped bead necklace 32
Cherry garland necklace 35
Threaded marshmallow necklace 38
Yo-yo necklace 40

CHAPTER 2
BRACELETS AND BANGLES 44
Cardboard tube bracelets 46
Felt and shell bracelets 48
Friendship bracelets 52
Stretchy button bracelets 56
Bracelet trio with ribbon 58
Fabric-wrapped bangles 60
Wire bead bracelet 63
Dachshund cuff 66
Zigzag bracelets 70
Ankle bells 72

CHAPTER 3
BROOCHES AND CORSAGES 76
Paper corsage 78
Sheriff's badge 80
Slate brooch 84
Felt flower brooches 86
Twinkling animal brooches 88
Tissue paper flower brooch 91
Cupcake brooch 94

CHAPTER 4
HAIR AND BAG ACCESSORIES 98
Fuzzy dinosaur badge 100
Pompom bag charm 102
Sequinned hair band 106
Tassel bag charm 109
Button hair barrette 112
Candy hair clips 114

Your jewelry crafting box 118
Techniques 119
Templates 124
Suppliers and resources 127
Acknowledgments 127
Index 128

Introduction

Adding brightness and sparkle to everyday clothes is fun! Dressing up is fun! And it's all much more fun if you make your own jewelry to jazz up your outfits.

Jewelry making is a great hobby because you can create beautiful, colorful accessories quickly and easily, using inexpensive materials, and without needing much space to do it—you could even make a friendship bracelet in a bus or car on your way to school!

My First Jewelry Making Book is full of exciting ideas to get you started with making jewelry, either to wear yourself or to give as gifts to your friends. The projects are sorted into four chapters to help you find exactly what you want to make. The chapters are: Necklaces and Pendants; Bracelets and Bangles; Brooches and Corsages; and Hair and Bag Accessories. There is something for everybody—from a sophisticated silk necklace to a marshmallow one you can eat!

Most of these projects are very simple, but to help you know where to start, we have graded them with one, two, or three smiley faces. Level one projects are simple and quick. Level two projects are a little more difficult and take a little longer. Level three projects will require you to use techniques which are more challenging, such as sewing and embroidery.

There is a techniques section which includes a list of materials you will need to get started (many of them you can find in your craft cupboard or around the house) and complete instructions for skills you will need, such as tying knots or how to sew the different stitches used in the projects.

So now it's time to get going on your very first piece of jewelry. What is it going to be?

Project levels

Level 1
These are quick and easy projects.

Level 2
These projects are quite easy but take a little longer to complete.

Level 3
These projects use advanced techniques and may need help from an adult.

Chapter 1

Necklaces and Pendants

Felt and wooden bead necklace 10

Salt dough beads 12

Felt bead necklace 16

Seed necklace 19

Rainbow felted necklace 22

Shell pendant 24

Raffia and bead necklace 26

Colorful clay pendant 28

Fabric-wrapped bead necklace 32

Cherry garland necklace 35

Threaded marshmallow necklace 38

Yo-yo necklace 40

Felt and wooden bead necklace

Make a necklace of plain wooden beads more interesting by adding in felt flowers. Finish it with a dainty velvet bow. These strong, bright colors look great worn over a plain T-shirt.

You will need

Strong thread for threading

1 small wooden bead

Large needle for threading

35 wooden beads

9 felt flowers

3 felt beads

Scissors

6 inches (15 cm) narrow velvet ribbon

1 Push the end of the thread through the hole in the small wooden bead. Pull the bead along so it is about 3 inches (8 cm) from the end, then tie a knot with the bead inside it. This will stop the other beads from slipping off the end of the thread while you are stringing them.

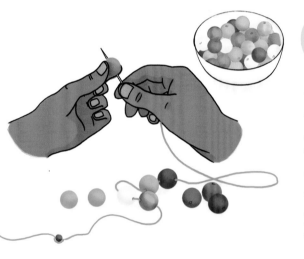

2 Thread the needle onto the other end of the thread. Thread five of the wooden beads in assorted colors onto the necklace. You may want to keep to the same order each time—e.g. red, blue, green, yellow, pink—or you may want to keep it random.

3 When you have added five wooden beads, thread a felt flower, followed by another five wooden beads. Then thread a felt flower, a felt bead, followed by another felt flower. Add another five wooden beads, followed by a single felt flower and repeat until you have strung on all the beads and flowers. Leave approximately 3 inches (8 cm) of thread free at the end for tying the necklace.

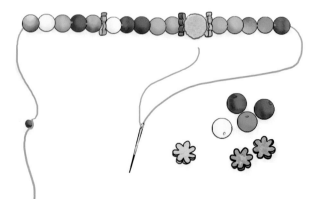

A quick, COLORFUL necklace

4

Tie the ends of the thread together in a double knot. Trim the ends with scissors.

5

Wrap the ribbon around the knots in the necklace and tie it in a bow. Trim the ribbon ends on the diagonal to prevent them from fraying.

Salt dough beads

Salt dough is a really good material for making big, chunky beads that you can paint in bright colors and then decorate. You don't need to make enough for a whole necklace—a few chunky beads arranged on a pretty ribbon look lovely.

You will need

1 cup (300 g) salt

Scant 1 cup (200 ml) lukewarm water

2¼ cups (300 g) all-purpose (plain) flour

1 tablespoon vegetable oil

Mixing bowl and wooden spoon

Measuring cup (jug)

Non-stick baking sheet

Table knife

Wooden skewer

Water-based paints and paintbrushes

Yarn or narrow ribbon

Large-eyed blunt needle

1 Put the salt into the mixing bowl, pour in the water and keep mixing until all the salt is dissolved and the water is clear.

2 Add the flour and the oil. Stir everything together until the mixture is too stiff to stir any more, then knead it with your hands to form a firm dough. Scrape the bowl clean and make the dough into a ball. It will be quite sticky. If the flour hasn't all mixed in, add a little more water.

3 Sprinkle plenty of flour onto the work surface and place the ball of dough onto it. Keep kneading it by pushing and folding it, until it is smooth, soft, and easy to mold.

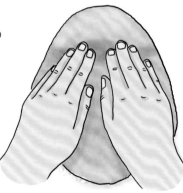

4 Take small pieces of dough and roll them in your hands to make bead shapes. Try to make them smooth all over. They can be all different shapes and sizes. Flatten some balls to make discs and cut off the sides of some with a table knife to make cube shapes.

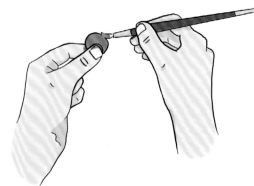

5 Push the skewer through the center of each bead to make a hole. Make the hole slightly bigger than you need as it will shrink a little when the salt dough is baked. Lay the beads on a baking sheet and ask an adult to help you put them in an oven at the lowest heat and bake them for about 1½ hours. After this time, ask an adult to turn the oven off, but leave the beads inside to cool completely. This slow cooling helps to stop the salt dough cracking.

Top tip!

....

You could paint the beads with PVA glue to make them shiny.

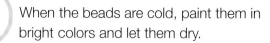

6 When the beads are cold, paint them in bright colors and let them dry.

7 When they are dry, decorate the beads with spots, flowers, and patterns in contrasting colors and again let them dry.

8 Cut a length of yarn that is long enough to fit over your head, adding extra for the knot. Design how the beads will be arranged and then thread the needle with the yarn and thread on the beads. Finally, take the needle off the yarn and tie the ends of the necklace with a double knot.

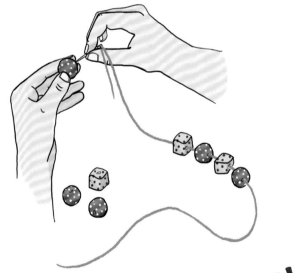

Designer beads DESIGNED by YOU!

Felt bead necklace

Colorful spirals of felt make gorgeous beads. Simply roll pieces of felt together into a sausage shape, add glue, and then cut them into slices. Play around with different color combinations and then thread them onto some cord to make fun necklaces and bracelets.

You will need

Squared paper

Felt sheets in different colors

Felt glue

Rubber bands

Sharp scissors

Ruler

Sharp needle

Embroidery floss (thread)

1 Cut out one rectangle measuring 5 x 4 inches (12 x 10 cm) and another measuring 5 x 3 inches (12 x 8 cm) from the squared paper. Use these as templates to cut out rectangles from two different colors of felt. Make sure that you put the template right into a corner of the felt so you don't waste any.

2 Lay the smaller rectangle onto the larger so that the two 5-inch (12-cm) widths match up and there is a small gap at each end. Spread glue along the gap at one end.

 3 Roll up the felt tightly, starting at the glued end.

4 When you have almost reached the end, holding the roll together with one hand, spread glue along the remaining edge with the other and stick the roll together. You need to keep it held together until the glue has dried. The easiest way to do this is with some rubber bands.

5 When the glue is completely dry, cut the felt roll into beads, making each one about ¾ inch (2 cm) wide. You will need sharp scissors. (You may need to ask an adult to help you with this.) Use the paper templates to cut out more rectangles of felt in different colors and repeat the gluing and rolling to make a pile of colorful beads.

6 Thread the needle with some embroidery floss (thread). The floss (thread) must be long enough to go over your head with a bit extra for tying it together. Knot one end to stop the beads slipping off and thread the beads on. If you push the needle through the center of the spiral you won't see the different colors so, for most of the beads, push it through from one side to the other. You'll have to push hard to get through all the layers! Try not to put beads of the same color next to each other. Finish with a double knot.

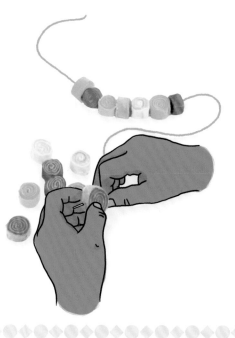

Seed necklace

When you carve out your Halloween pumpkin or when you next make pumpkin soup, don't throw away the seeds. Make them into a necklace instead. This one uses sycamore seeds as well, for variety, or you could add in some wooden beads.

You will need

Pumpkin
Spoon
Bowl of warm water
Strainer (colander)
Tray
Dish towel (tea towel)
Sharp needle
Cotton thread
Sycamore seeds

1 Ask an adult to help you cut the top off the pumpkin. Using a spoon, loosen the pumpkin flesh around the seeds and then scoop out the fibers and seeds from the middle, using your hands.

2 Put all the seeds in a bowl of warm water and leave to soak for a couple of hours (you could carve your pumpkin in the meantime). After this, the fibers will come away from the seeds. Carefully pick out the seeds one by one and put them in a strainer (colander).

Use every part of your **PUMPKIN!**

3 When all the seeds are in the colander, run it under a faucet (tap) to remove any remaining bits of sticky orange fiber.

4 Cover a tray with a clean dish towel (tea towel). Carefully, lay out the seeds so they are not touching each other. Leave the tray in a warm dry place until the seeds have dried out. This can take up to a week.

5 When the seeds are dry, cut a long piece of cotton thread. Thread the needle and tie a big double knot at the end. Check that the thread is long enough to go over your head with enough extra to tie a knot at the back of the necklace. Begin threading the seeds onto the needle. Be careful not to prick yourself when you pierce the seeds! Every so often add in a sycamore seed or a wooden bead.

Top tips!

Make matching bracelets: cut shorter lengths of fine elastic and thread on the pumpkin seeds then knot the ends. These make great presents!

Paint the pumpkin seeds in a variety of pretty colors after they have been dried.

seed necklace **21**

Rainbow felted necklace

This necklace mixes up pretty wooden beads with squares of colored felt. You can make felt from old woolen blankets or sweaters or you can use felt from the craft store. This necklace is threaded onto elastic so it can be quite short and still fit over your head.

You will need

Squared paper

Old woolen blankets or sweaters (see Tip) or colored felt

Pointed needle with a large eye

Beading elastic $\frac{1}{32}$ inch (0.8 mm) thick, approximately 36 inches (80 cm) long

16 flat round wooden beads (spacer beads)—all in one color

8 large oval wooden beads—all in one color

Scissors

1 If you have some old woolen blankets or moth eaten sweaters ask an adult to wash them for you on a really hot wash in the washing machine. This will turn the wool into felt. If you can't do this, use ordinary felt from the craft store.

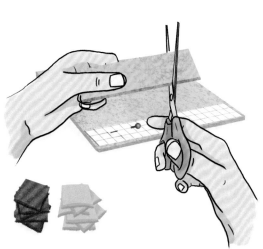

2 Cut a strip of squared paper that is ¾ inch (2 cm) wide and as long as possible. Pin this to the felt and use it as a template to cut out a strip of felt. Now cut the felt strip into squares. Keep doing this on different colored felts. You need 8 sets of 12 squares, so you need to do a lot of cutting but you can repeat colors.

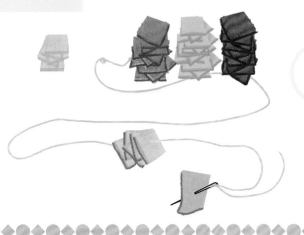

3 Thread the needle with the elastic. Tie a double knot in the end and then thread on 12 pieces of felt in your first color. Try to push the needle through the middle of the square.

Top tip!

You can sometimes find old woolen blankets or sweaters in thrift (charity) stores.

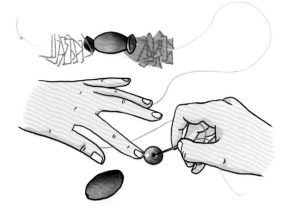

4 Now thread on a round spacer bead, followed by a large oval bead, and another spacer. Next, thread on 12 more pieces of felt in a different color, followed by spacer bead, oval bead, spacer bead.

5 Keep going until you have used up all the beads—you should have eight sets of felt squares. Knot the ends of the elastic together with a double knot.

Shell pendant

Boys like jewelry, too, and this shell pendant would be a perfect present for a brother or friend. You need shells or smallish flat pebbles with holes in them, so remember to look for some when you next go to the beach. Large flat oyster shells like these are perfect for painting. Paint on different designs: fish or little boats work well, and this brightly colored skull is based on Mexican folk art.

You will need

Flat shells or pebbles with holes

Felt-tipped pens or paints in assorted colors

Metallic gold or silver pen

Waxed cotton beading thread (or a long shoe lace would do)

1 Make sure your shell is clean and dry. Paint or draw a design onto your shell—a bold shape will stand out clearly. (You may wish to use the templates on page 124.)

2 Add some decoration using a metallic pen to make it sparkle.

Super **COOL** pendant

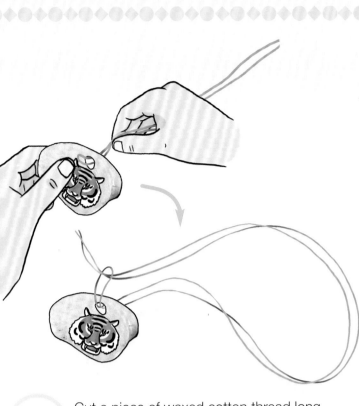

3 Cut a piece of waxed cotton thread long enough to go easily over your head and with about 1½ inches (4 cm) extra for tying knots. Fold the thread in half and thread the two ends through the hole in the shell and back through the loop in the thread. Pull tightly to secure.

4 Tie a knot in the two strands above the pendant and tie in another shell or small stone above the knot, tying a reef knot (see page 122) firm up against it so it can't slip out. Add another shell in the same way if you wish. Tie the two ends of the thread together to finish the pendant.

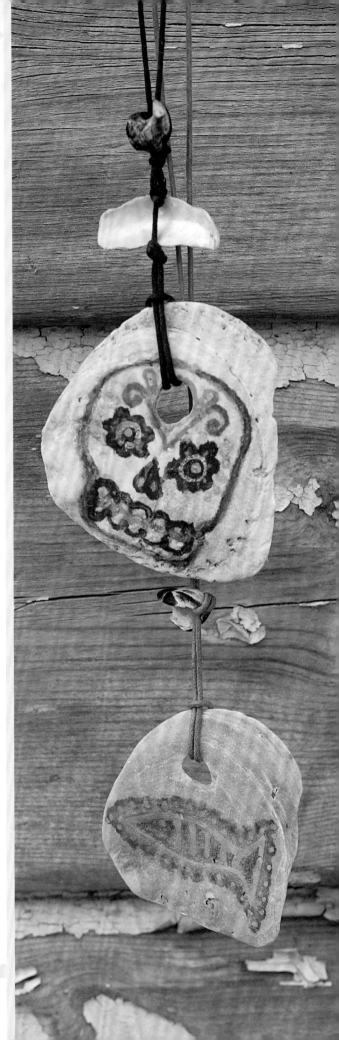

Raffia and bead necklace

This bright, knobbly, knotty necklace is made with raffia and wooden beads. Raffia is a natural material which is straw-colored but you can get it dyed in really bright colors, too.

You will need

1 reel of raffia

Scissors

Approximately 15 chunky wooden beads, in assorted colors and shapes

1 Cut two equal lengths of raffia, each about 32 inches (80 cm) long. You need it this long to start with as it quickly becomes shorter as you thread and knot in your beads. Tie a knot in the two pieces of raffia about 3 inches (8 cm) from the end.

2 Thread a bead through one strand of the raffia. The other strand goes around the outside of the bead. Knot the two strands together again underneath the bead.

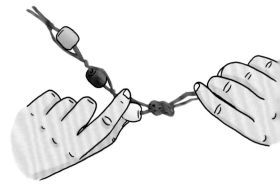

3 Keep going like this, threading a bead onto one strand and knotting the two strands together, until the necklace is long enough to fit over your head when tied into a loop. You will need to have 3 inches (8 cm) of the raffia left to tie the ends together. Tie the two ends with a double knot.

A KNOBBLY, KNOTTY necklace

Colorful clay pendant

By rolling or twisting different colors of modeling clay together, you can make these fun, chunky pendants and beads.

You will need

Parchment paper

Modeling clay (such as Fimo) in at least 2 different colors

Rolling pin

Different shaped cookie cutters

Wooden skewer

Baking sheet lined with parchment paper

20 inches (50 cm) satin ribbon, ⅛ inch (3 mm) wide

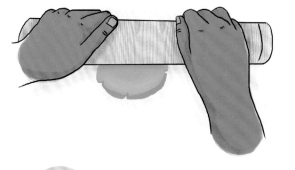

1 Cover a work surface with parchment paper. This will protect the surface as well as stop the clay from sticking. Take a piece of clay and roll it flat with your rolling pin. It needs to be about ⅛ inch (3 mm) thick.

2 Take tiny pieces of clay in a different color. Roll them into balls which are a little smaller than a pea. Place them on top of the flat piece of clay and then roll over the surface with your rolling pin so that the balls are flattened into spots and become part of the bottom piece.

3 Place the cookie cutter onto the clay and push it down firmly to cut out the heart or flower shape.

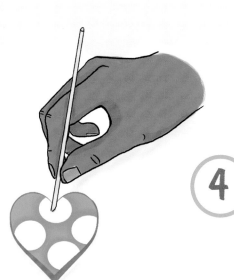

4 Make a hole at the top of the pendant with the wooden skewer and place it on the lined baking sheet.

5 To make the stripy bead, take two small pieces of clay in different colors (you can use the same two as you used for the pendant or choose two different ones). Roll each piece into a small sausage. Press the two sausages together and then, holding them at either end, twist them together to create a spiral pattern.

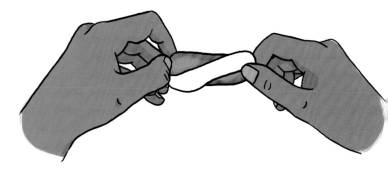

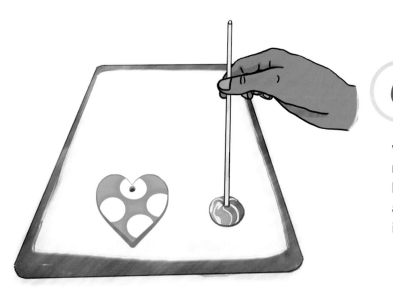

6 Take a lump of the stripy clay and roll it into a smooth ball between your palms. Push a wooden skewer through the middle to make a hole. Put the bead onto the baking sheet with the pendant. Ask an adult to bake it in the oven following the instructions on the packet.

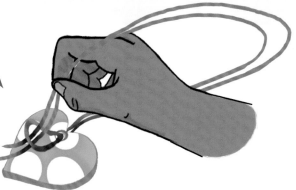

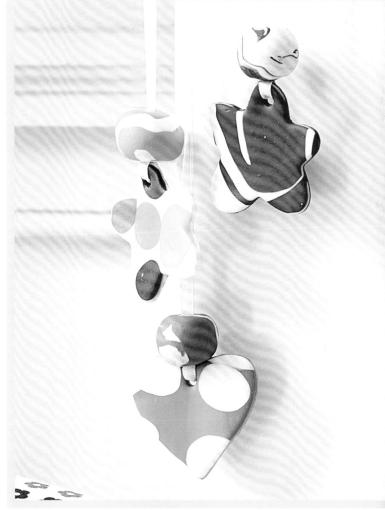

7 When the bead and pendant have cooled, thread them onto the ribbon. Fold the ribbon in half and thread the two ends through the hole in the pendant. Then thread them back through the loop in the thread and pull up tight. Add on the bead, threading both ends of the ribbon through the bead.

8 Tie the two ends of ribbon in a bow or knot to finish your necklace.

Make CLEVER PATTERNS in CLAY

Fabric-wrapped bead necklace

Transform simple beads into something very special by covering them in pretty patterned fabrics. Use up material from old dresses that are too tatty to take to the thrift (charity) store or buy off-cuts at your local fabric store. Each bead might remind you of a favorite dress! The fabric needs to be quite fine or the beads will look lumpy.

You will need

20 inches (50 cm) colored cotton cord

Toggle clasp

Sharp scissors

Scraps of fabric in different patterns and colors

Glue stick

7 large wooden beads

Assorted small round and barrel-shaped wooden beads

1 Tie one end of the cord to either the ring or bar of the toggle clasp. Secure with a double knot and cut the end off short.

2 With sharp scissors, cut small, narrow strips of fabric, long enough to wrap right around one of the large beads.

TRANSFORM an ordinary bead!

3 Take a strip of material and cover the back all over with glue, taking care to glue right over the edges.

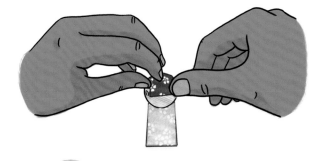

4 Starting at the top, wrap the glued strip around a large bead and smooth it over to remove any creases.

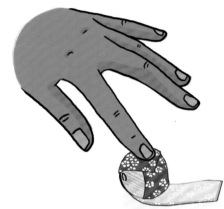

5 Glue and stick on another strip in the same way, but at a slight diagonal to the first, so that you are covering over more of the bead. Keep sticking on strips until the whole bead is covered, taking care not to glue fabric over the holes. Cover all of the large beads in this way and let them dry completely.

6 Start threading beads onto your cord. Begin with about 13 small beads, then add in a fabric bead, then another small bead, then another fabric bead. Keep going with alternate fabric and small beads until all the fabric beads have been threaded. Now match the 13 beads you threaded first, with another 13 small beads to make the necklace symmetrical.

7 Tie the second piece of the toggle fastening to the cord so the necklace will fasten together. Use a double knot and cut off the long end of cord.

Cherry garland necklace

Yummy, gummy, cherry candies! Tie them in knots and wear them to look beautiful—then you can eat them!

1 Lay the cherries in a line so that the colors match, red cherry to red cherry and green stalk to green stalk. Make sure that there is a green stalk at both ends of the line.

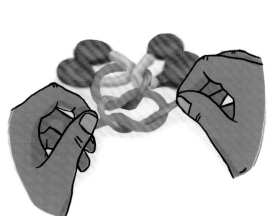

2 Cut a piece of green candy string to about 6 inches (15 cm) long. Loop it through two of the green stalks to tie them together. Tie the ends in a reef knot (see page 122). Pull both ends tight and trim the ends off short. (Eat the trimmings!) Repeat this for all the other pairs of green stalks—but don't tie the end ones together.

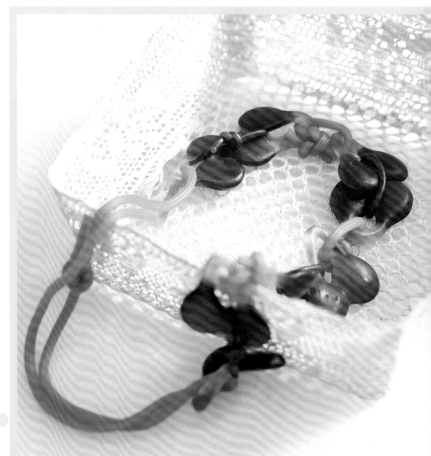

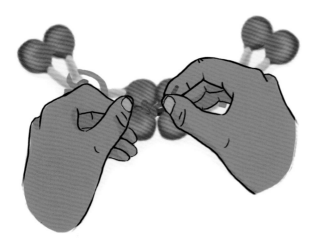

 3 Now link the red cherries together in the same way by using sections of strawberry laces.

YUMMY gummy CHERRY candies!

4 When all the cherries are linked together, take one long length of the green string, loop it through both ends of the cherry chain, and tie it in a reef knot, trimming the ends to make them neat.

Threaded marshmallow necklace

Make these soft, squidgy, marshmallow necklaces as a fun activity for a birthday party. See if you can find different types of marshmallow—some big, some small, some striped, some in different shapes—so you and your guests can create patterns in the necklaces. Everyone can tie them on to take home.

You will need

Strawberry or licorice laces

Marshmallows in different shapes and sizes

Large-eyed blunt needle

1 Sort the marshmallows into different bowls for different shapes, sizes, and colors.

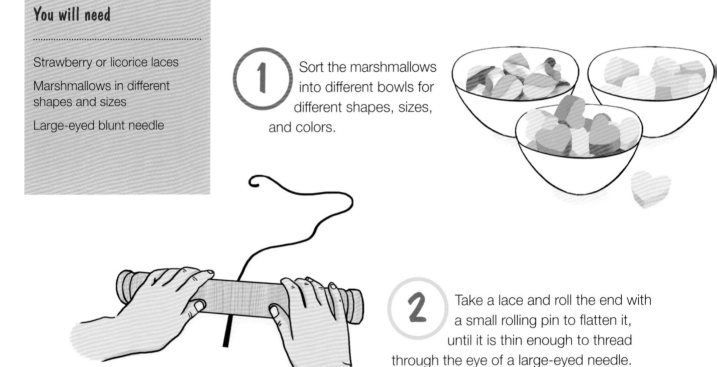

2 Take a lace and roll the end with a small rolling pin to flatten it, until it is thin enough to thread through the eye of a large-eyed needle.

3 Now thread on the marshmallows. Leave enough room at the ends to tie a knot so that you can tie the necklace around your neck. Now wear, eat, and enjoy!

Yo-yo necklace

This is a very special necklace made out of pretty silk fabrics, buttons, and beads, but any fine fabric will do. You can make it more sparkly and elaborate by sewing on more beads or just keep it simple.

You will need

Small pieces of 3 different fine fabrics

Round objects to draw around such as a CD, a coffee mug, and a small glass

Pencil

Scissors

4 heart-shaped buttons

Assorted small beads

15 inches (37.5 cm) beading thread

1 set of necklace fastenings

1 You need to find three different sized round objects to draw round—a CD is a good size for the largest, a coffee mug for one a bit smaller, and a glass that's a bit smaller than the coffee mug for the third. Draw round the CD on one fabric, round the coffee mug twice on another, and round the glass twice on the third fabric. Cut out these five circles.

2 Lay one circle right side down on an ironing board and ask an adult to help you turn over the edge of the fabric by about ⅛ inch (3 mm) all the way round each circle and iron it flat. Do the same for the other four circles.

3 Thread the needle with a length of thread. Sew a few small stitches over and over at the edge of one of the circles so that the thread is firmly attached. Now sew small neat running stitches all the way round the edge of the circle, sewing where the fabric is turned in so that you are sewing through two layers. (This is to keep the edge neat.)

4 At the end, keep the needle threaded and carefully pull the thread to gather up the yo-yo. Then sew a few small stitches over and over in the same place so the yo-yo doesn't come undone. Cut the thread and flatten the yo-yo. Make yo-yos with the other circles in the same way.

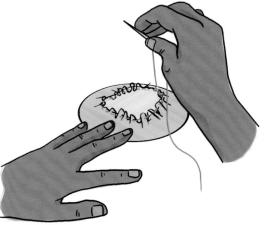

5 Arrange the yo-yos with the largest in the middle, the medium-sized ones either side of it, and the smaller ones at each end. Arrange them in a curve.

6 Take the middle yo-yo and stitch the ones at either side to it, looping the thread over and over between them and finishing as before. Then stitch on the two outside ones. Make sure that you keep the curve.

7 Stitch a heart-shaped button over the stitches between each yo-yo. (This looks pretty and hides the stitches.) If you wish, you could also stitch on some beads in the center of each yo-yo.

8 Now thread your needle with some beading thread or other strong thread. Attach the thread to one side of the yo-yos, again looping the thread over and over several times to make sure that it is firmly attached.

9 Thread on beads in colors to match your yo-yos. Hold the necklace up against your neck to find out when it is long enough.

10 Push the needle through the loop on one end of the necklace fastening and secure the thread with a double knot. Do the same on the other side of the yo-yo, making sure that you have the same number of beads on each side to make the necklace symmetrical.

Chapter 2
Bracelets and Bangles

Cardboard tube bracelets 46

Felt and shell bracelets 48

Friendship bracelets 52

Stretchy button bracelets 56

Bracelet trio with ribbon 58

Fabric-wrapped bangles 60

Wire bead bracelet 63

Dachshund cuff 66

Zigzag bracelets 70

Ankle bells 72

Cardboard tube bracelets

Who would think that you could make jewelry from toilet paper tubes—but that's what these pretty bracelets are made from! Paint them in zingy colors and decorate them with ribbons and buttons.

You will need

Cardboard tubes

Scissors

Ruler

Paint

Paintbrush

Ricrac braid and ribbon

PVA glue

Buttons

1 Cut open the cardboard tube in a straight line using scissors. Then measure 2 inches (5 cm) in from the bottom of the cardboard roll and make a mark. Do this in four or five different places around the roll and then join up the dots to make a straight line. Cut along this line to make a single bracelet. Be careful not to flatten the roll as you draw and cut.

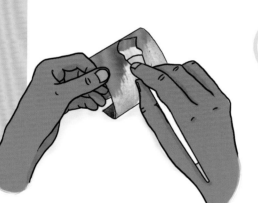

2 Paint the cardboard roll both inside and out with your chosen color of paint and let it dry thoroughly. (If it is still patchy, paint on a second coat and let it dry.) When it is dry, paint a layer of PVA glue over the paint—this will varnish it and stop the paint coming off onto your wrist. Let it dry.

3 Measure around the bracelet with the ribbon and cut it to the right size. Cut the ricrac braid to the same length. Run a line of glue along the ribbon and stick it in place around the bracelet. Smooth out any wrinkles. Do the same for the ricrac.

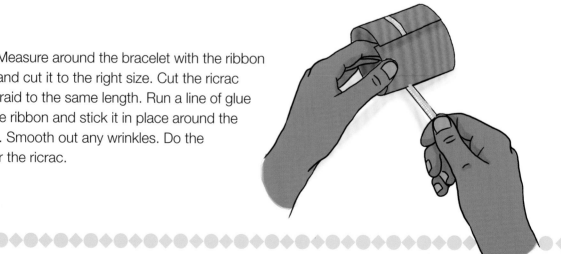

4 Once the glue is completely dry, stick a row of buttons around the top and bottom edge of the bracelet. Stick just a few at a time and then wait for them to dry before sticking more. If you try and glue them all at once they may slide off when you turn the bracelet around.

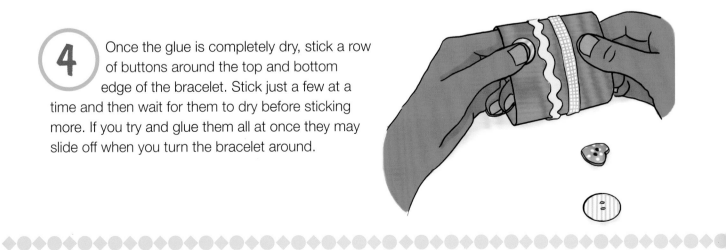

Felt and shell bracelets

Beaches are covered with treasures—from huge pieces of driftwood to tiny fragments of shells worn smooth by the sea. You can find these tiny shell pieces in many different colors—from pearly pinks and oranges to deep blues and purples. Placed together in a row, they make a pretty and very unusual bracelet.

You will need

Felt

Scissors

Fragments of shells

Small shell with a hole in it (for making a fastening)

Sewing needle and thread

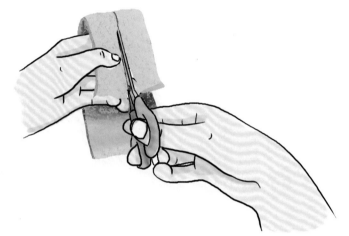

1 Measure and cut a strip of felt about ⅝ inch (1.5 cm) wide. For the length, wrap the strip around your wrist and add about ¾ inch (2 cm) overlap. Mark it and then trim off any extra.

2 Thread the needle with a long length of thread, double it over, and knot it with a double knot.

3 Start sewing on the first shell fragment about 1 inch (2.5 cm) from one end. Pull the needle up from the back of the felt, cross it over the shell, and push it down the other side. Hold the shell in place while you pull the needle up through the felt again, further round the shell. Cross it over the shell and down again to make a cross. Do this again, so that you have a star pattern of threads over the shell fragment holding it so it can't slip out.

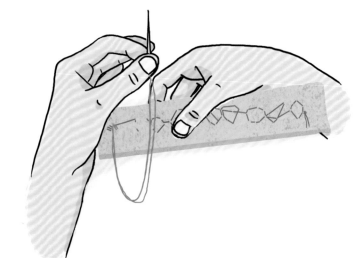

4 Pull the thread under the felt to the position of the next fragment and sew this one on in the same way. Space the shells evenly. When you are running out of thread make a few small stitches over and over on top of each other on the back of the felt, behind the shell. This will secure the thread. Then trim the ends. The last shell should be ¾ inch (2 cm) from the end. Secure your thread behind this shell, too, before you cut the needle off.

5 Fold the ¾-inch (2-cm) end piece over and snip a little slit in the center of the felt. Try not to get the slit too near the edge.

Tiny TREASURES from the sea

6 Finally, find a small shell which has some holes in it which you can sew on, like a button, through the holes. Sew this onto the opposite end to the slit, as the fastening button. If you can't find a suitable shell, sew a small button on instead (see page 122).

Friendship bracelets

These braided bracelets are so easy and quick to make that you will be creating them for all your friends in no time. Any yarn (wool) or braid can be used, but remember that the chunkier the yarn, the thicker the bracelet will be.

You will need

Yarn (wool) in 2 colors

Bulldog clip

Cardboard

Scissors

Small beads (optional)

1 Cut three lengths of yarn each 27 inches (70 cm) long from one color of yarn. Choose another color which you think will look good with it and cut three more lengths of this yarn.

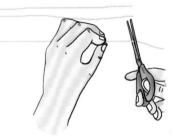

2 Put all six lengths of yarn together and tie them in a knot about 2 inches (5 cm) from one end.

3 Hold the knotted end of the yarn firm by clipping it to the top of a piece of cardboard. Separate the colors so that three strands of the same color are on the left and three strands of the other color are on the right. Take the left-hand strands and loop them over the right-hand strands.

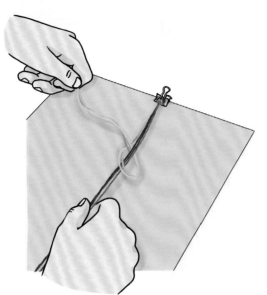

4 Pull the left-hand strands back through the loop and tighten into a knot that sits right against your first knot, all the while holding the right-hand bundle straight.

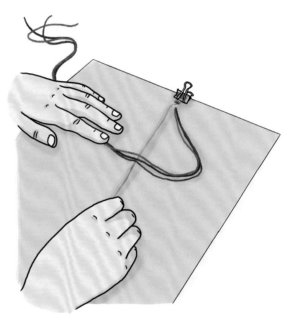

5 Now straighten the left-hand bundle and loop the right-hand bundle over it.

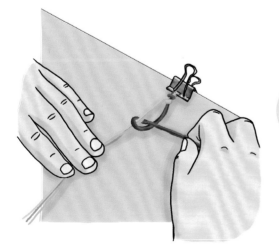

6 Pull it back through the loop that you have just made and tighten in the same way as you did before, again holding the other yarn strands straight.

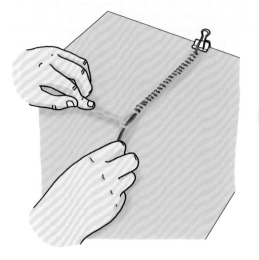

7 Keep going like this, left then right, until the bracelet is long enough to fit around your friend's wrist.

8 Unclip the bracelet from the wooden board and tie the ends into a knot.

9 If you want to, thread beads onto some of the individual strands for extra decoration, tying the ends of the yarn into large knots to hold the beads in place.

Make a friend HAPPY

Stretchy button bracelets

Buttons and beads go well together to make this easy bracelet. Raid the family button box for all those extra buttons taken off clothes that have long ago gone to the thrift (charity) store. You can choose buttons in shades of one color or go for all the colors of the rainbow. Space the buttons out with pretty beads.

You will need

About 20 buttons in varying sizes

20 small round beads

Length of thin elastic cord, about 10 inches (25 cm) long

Scissors

1 Tie a knot about 2 inches (5 cm) from the end of the elastic so the beads won't drop off the end.

2 Thread the beads and buttons alternately onto the elastic until the beads and buttons fit around your wrist—you may not need them all.

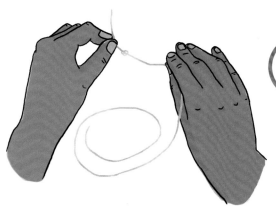

3 Tie the two ends together in a double knot or reef knot (see page 122) and trim off the excess elastic with scissors.

Buttons and BEADS!

Bracelet trio with ribbon

Three bracelets joined together with a bow look really pretty. Make all the bracelets very different—have one all plain, one in shades of the same color, and one with a sequence of different colored beads.

You will need

Length of thin elastic cord, about 30 inches (75 cm) long

Scissors

Assorted glass or plastic beads

6 inches (15 cm) satin ribbon

1 Plan which beads you will use for each bracelet and sort them into three dishes ready to use.

2 Measure and cut a length of elastic 10 inches (25 cm) long for your first bracelet. Use this first length of elastic as a guide and cut two more of the same length.

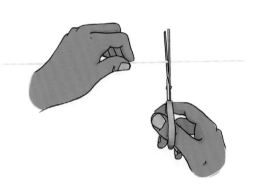

3 Tie a knot in the elastic about 2 inches (5 cm) from the end so that the beads won't fall off when you are threading. Decide which beads you will use for your first bracelet and thread the beads onto the elastic. Check to see that there are enough beads threaded to fit around your wrist and then tie the two ends together in a double knot or reef knot (see page 122) and cut off any excess elastic.

(**4**) Thread and finish the other two bracelets in the same way, measuring them up against the first one to be sure that they are all the same size. When you have finished all three bracelets, group them together. Hold each of them by the knots so the knots line up. Wrap the ribbon around all three, where the knots are, and tie the ribbon in a firm knot. Then finish with a bow.

bracelet trio with ribbon **59**

Fabric-wrapped bangles

Buy some plain, plastic bangles and make them into something really special by covering them in fabric. Cotton fabrics with dainty flower patterns or polka dots work well. You could use fabrics from old clothes that are too worn out to go to the thrift (charity) store or buy some remnants.

You will need

Lengths of patterned fabric, at least 24 inches (60 cm) long

Narrow ruler, about 1 inch (2.5 cm) wide

Pencil

Scissors

Plastic bangles

Glue stick or PVA glue

Ribbon (optional)

1 Spread out the fabric with the wrong side facing up on a table. Place the ruler on the fabric with one side against the long straight edge of the fabric. Draw along the other edge to give you a strip a ruler's width wide. When you reach the end of the ruler, move it along and keep drawing until the strip is 24 inches (60 cm) long.

2 Cut along the line to create a strip of fabric.

3 Take the end of your fabric strip and, making sure the right side of the fabric is facing you, glue it to the inside of your bangle. Let it dry for a few minutes. (PVA glue will take longer, but it will be stronger.)

 4 Begin to wrap the fabric strip tightly around the bangle, making sure it overlaps each time and that none of the plastic bangle is showing through. Continue wrapping until all the bangle is covered with fabric.

5 When you have finished wrapping the bangle, cut off any excess fabric, cutting it so that there is about 1 inch (2.5 cm) spare for gluing on the inside of the bangle.

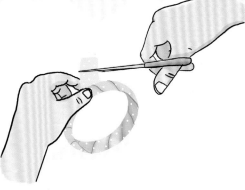

6 Apply glue to the end of the fabric strip. PVA glue is better for this. If you are using a glue stick, make sure that you put on plenty of glue. Stick the end to the inside of the bangle so it is invisible when you are wearing it. Let it dry.

7 Trim off any stray bits of fabric that may have frayed while you were wrapping.

8 Make more bangles in different fabrics and tie them together with a ribbon bow.

Cute cotton-covered BANGLES

Wire bead bracelet

This delicate bracelet is made by rolling thin wire around beads, creating an eye-catching effect. The technique is so simple and the result so beautiful, you may want to make a necklace to match. Use brightly colored beads that will shine through the wire mesh. You can use softer colored beads in between the wire beads—try using faceted ones to add some extra sparkle.

You will need :

2 reels of thin wire, 1/16 inch (2 mm) thick

Scissors

7 large beads

Toggle clasp

8 smaller faceted beads

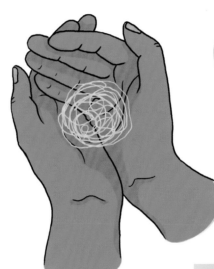

1 Cut a length of wire 3 feet (1 m) long. Using circular motions, gently roll the wire in the palm of your hand to make it into a ball shape.

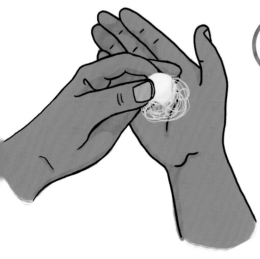

2 When the wire starts to look like a ball, drop a large bead into the middle and continue rolling until the wire is wrapped tightly around the bead. Wrap all of the seven large beads in this way.

Metal **MAGIC**

3 Cut another piece of wire 10 inches (25 cm) long for threading the beads. First, thread 1 inch (2.5 cm) of the wire through the small ring on the toggle ring, then bend it back and twist it around the long end of wire to secure the ring in place.

4 Now thread the beads onto the wire—first a small faceted bead, then a wire-covered bead, then a faceted one. Keep going in this pattern.

5 When you have only 2 inches (5 cm) of wire left, stop threading beads and thread the small ring on the toggle bar onto the end of the wire. Pull the wire tight, making sure that the beads have no gaps between them.

6 Thread the wire over the ring on the toggle bar and back up through it, to hold the toggle bar in place. Do this a few times to make sure it is secure. Trim off the end of the wire with a pair of scissors.

Dachshund cuff

This delightful dachshund will spend many happy hours chasing its own tail around your wrist. The cuff is more difficult than many of the projects in this book and will allow you to practice your embroidery stitches.

You will need

Templates on page 124

Squared paper

Brown felt, approximately 2½ x 6 inches (6 x 15 cm)

Small piece of dark brown felt

Yellow felt, approximately 2¾ x 6¾ inches (7 x 17 cm)

Blue felt, approximately 2¾ x 6¾ inches (7 x 17 cm)

Brown, dark brown, black, blue, and yellow sewing threads

Purple, blue, and black stranded embroidery flosses (threads)

Black seed bead

Black elastic, ¼ inch (5 mm) wide, approximately 4 inches (10 cm) long

Needles, scissors, pins

1 Trace the templates on page 124 and cut them out. Pin the dog shape to the brown felt and cut round it. Pin the ear shape to the dark brown felt and cut round that. For the background, cut out a rectangle measuring 2 x 6 inches (5 x 15 cm) from the squared paper and use it as a template to cut out one yellow felt rectangle and one blue felt rectangle.

2 Pin the dachshund to the center of the yellow cuff piece, and sew around the edge with straight stitch (see page 121) in brown sewing thread. Sew the ear in place with straight stitch in dark brown sewing thread.

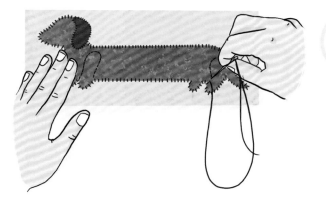

3 Cut out the front leg from the dachshund paper template along the dotted line and draw round it with pencil onto the felt body. Do the same for the back leg. Then use doubled dark brown thread to backstitch (see page 120) along the lines to mark the shapes of the legs on the dog's body.

4 Cut a length of black embroidery floss (thread) and separate half the strands (so for six-stranded floss, use three strands). Switch to a larger needle if necessary and sew a few long stitches close together to form the dog's nose. Use black sewing thread to backstitch a curved line to form the smile, and sew on a black seed bead for the eye. Sew the bead in place with three or four stitches, sewing it flat like an "O."

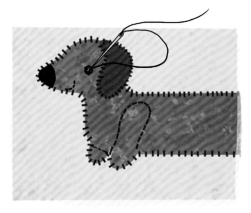

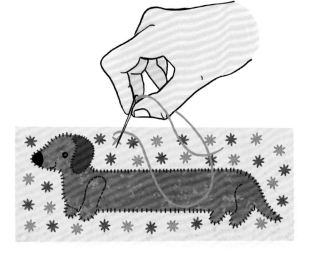

5 Fill in the empty space around the dachshund with small, embroidered blue and purple stars. Use half the strands of embroidery floss (as before), and sew four overlapping stitches to create each eight-pointed star (see page 121).

6 Cut two lengths of black elastic, each approximately 2 inches (5 cm) long. Sew the elastic to the blue cuff piece, positioning it so it overlaps the felt by about ⅜ inch (1 cm) at each end and stitching it in place with blue sewing thread. Sew both lengths of elastic to one end of the cuff and then fold the cuff around to make a circle. Try it to see how big it is and then sew the elastic to the other end to fit your wrist.

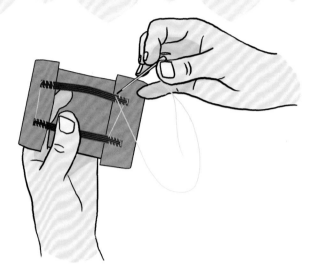

Can he EVER catch his TAIL?

7 Put the yellow dachshund felt piece over the blue piece with the ends of the elastic sandwiched between the two pieces and the dachshund on the outside. Pin the layers together. Sew the edges together with blanket stitch using yellow sewing thread (see page 121). Finish the stitching neatly on the inside of the cuff with a few stitches over and over each other in the same place. Trim the thread.

Zigzag bracelets

By braiding old-fashioned ricrac trim, you can make these excitingly different bracelets. They are simple to make but you do need proper bracelet fastenings to finish them off.

You will need

Ricrac trim in 3 different colors

Scissors

Sticky tape

Bulldog clip

Piece of scrap card

2 bracelet end caps

PVA glue

Jump ring

Bracelet catch

1 Cut a piece of ricrac trim, 8 inches (20 cm) long, from each of the three different colors. Wrap a narrow piece of sticky tape around the ends to hold the three pieces together.

2 Use the bulldog clip to clip the ends to the card to hold them firmly. Braid (plait) the ricrac (see page 123) using the zigzag shape as a guide for your braiding—the zigzags should slot comfortably into each other.

3 When you get to the end of the ricrac, wrap another narrow piece of sticky tape around the ends to hold them together. Check the bracelet is the correct size. It needs to be a little smaller than your wrist because the catch and rings will add to the length. If it is too big, trim off a little ricrac and tape the ends again.

Zany ZIGZAGS!

4 Place one taped end into a bracelet end cap. If the sticky tape shows beyond the edge of the cap, trim a little bit off the end of the bracelet so that the strip of tape is narrow enough to be hidden inside the cap. Repeat with the other end so you have a neat finish. Take the ends out again and squeeze glue into one of the end caps and push one end of the braid into the cap. Allow the glue to dry a little and go sticky before gluing the other end of the bracelet into the other end cap in the same way. Let the glue dry for at least 2 hours until it is completely set.

5 Use the jump ring to attach the bracelet catch to one of the end caps. You can ask an adult to help you do this with a pair of pliers, but you may find the jump ring is soft enough to open and close by hand.

Ankle bells

Once you are good at making friendship bracelets, why not try these ankle bells, which are just a little bit more tricky? Tie them on and you'll jingle as you dance.

You will need (for one anklet)

96 inches (2.4 m) yarn (wool)

Scissors

Bulldog clip

Scrap piece of cardboard

13 small craft bells, size ⁵⁄₁₆ inch (7.5 mm)

1 Cut two lengths of colorful yarn (wool), each one measuring approximately 48 inches (1.2 m). Fold the yarn in half and knot the folded ends of the yarn together to form a small loop.

2 Clip the yarn, by the loop, to the scrap piece of cardboard.

3 The anklets are made with square knots which are tricky when you first try them—keep going—they soon become easy. First bring the right strand over the two middle strands.

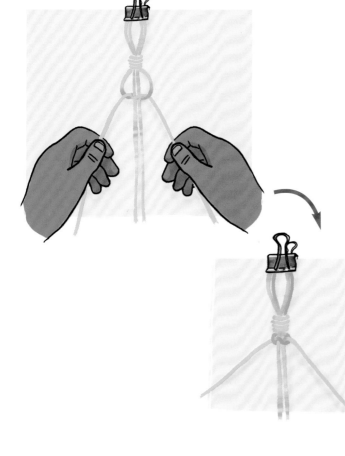

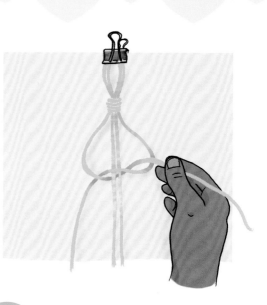

4 Bring the left strand over the right strand, under the two middle strands, and up through the loop formed by the right strand.

5 Pull the right and left strand until the knot tightens. It helps to hold the middle strands tight when you do this—maybe between your knees when you first start! Keep pulling until the knot is right up against your first knot.

Jingle as you DANCE!

6 Now do the same thing the other way round. Bring the left strand over the two middle strands. Then bring the right strand over the left strand, under the two middle strands, and up through the loop formed by the left strand. Hold the middle strands straight and pull the right and left strands until the knot tightens. This is your first completed square knot!

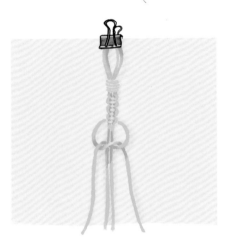

7 Repeat steps 5, 6, and 7 until you have tied four square knots. (Remember—each knot is made up of a part starting on the right and a part starting on the left.)

8 Now thread a bell onto the left-hand length of yarn and tie two more square knots. Add another bell and tie two more square knots. Keep going until you have used up all the bells. Finish with two square knots.

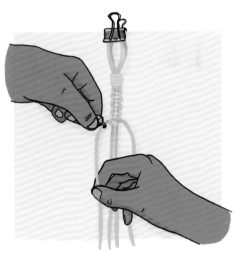

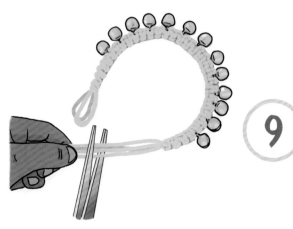

9 Trim the ends leaving about 2½ inches (6 cm) of yarn at the end. Fasten the anklets as you would a friendship bracelet.

Chapter 3

Brooches and Corsages

Paper corsage 78

Sheriff's badge 80

Slate brooch 84

Felt flower brooches 86

Twinkling animal brooches 88

Tissue paper flower brooch 91

Cupcake brooch 94

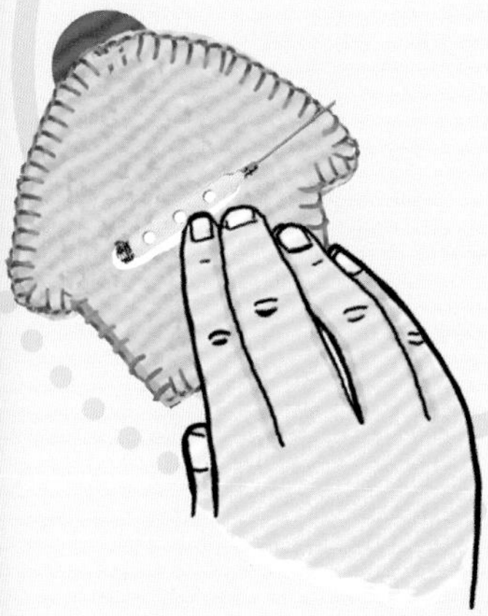

Paper corsage

This could either be a flowery brooch for you to wear on a dress or jacket, or a flower to decorate a special present to give to a friend. Use up all those ends of gift wrap which are too small to wrap presents. Glittery paper is great to use at Christmas time.

You will need

Decorative paper (such as gift wrap)

Pencil

Ruler

Scissors

Glue stick

1 decorative button

1 metal brooch back

PVA glue

Sticky tape

1 Using a pencil and ruler, mark four strips measuring ¾ x 8 inches (2 x 20 cm) on the back of your decorative paper. When you are measuring, mark the center of each strip with a dot. Cut out the strips with scissors.

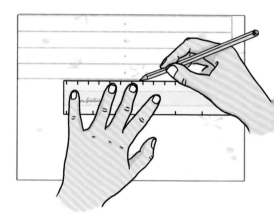

2 Lay the first strip on a flat surface with the patterned side facing down. Use the glue stick to put a little glue on the center mark. Lay the next strip on top, to make a cross, with the center marks lined up, then glue the center again. Lay the next two strips on in the same way, arranging the strips in a star shape.

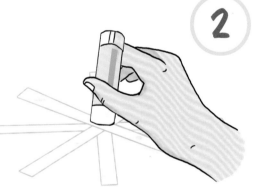

3 Fold in the end of one strip toward the center so that it forms a loop and stick it in place using the glue stick. Fold in the other end and stick it in place in the same way. The ends should overlap a little. Repeat with the other strips so that you make a looped flower shape. Let the glue dry for a few minutes.

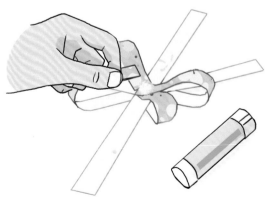

Lovely LOOPY flowers!

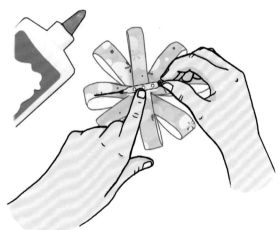

(4) Use PVA glue to stick a pretty button to the center of the flower corsage. Let it dry.

(5) If you are using the flower as a corsage, rather than for a parcel, you will need to stick on a brooch pin. Turn the flower corsage to the wrong side and stick on the metal brooch back using a blob of PVA glue. Make extra secure with a small piece of sticky tape.

Sheriff's badge

Make a sheriff's badge in girly pastels to dress up a line dancing outfit or use something brighter to give it a real Wild West feel. This could be a project for the boys or for girls who want to make a gift for their friend or brother!

You will need

1 cup (300 g) salt

Scant 1 cup (200 ml) lukewarm water

2¼ cups (300 g) all-purpose (plain) flour

1 tablespoon vegetable oil

Mixing bowl and wooden spoon

Measuring cup (jug)

Non-stick baking sheet

Star-shaped cookie cutter

Smaller round cookie cutter

Water-based paints and paintbrushes

PVA glue

Brooch pin

1 Put the salt into the mixing bowl, pour in the water, and keep mixing until all the salt has dissolved and the water is clear.

2 Add the flour and the oil. Stir everything together until the mixture is too stiff to stir any more, then knead it with your hands to form a firm dough. Scrape the bowl clean and make the dough into a ball. It will be quite sticky. If the flour hasn't all mixed in, add a little more water.

3 Sprinkle plenty of flour onto the work surface and place the ball of dough onto it. Keep kneading it by pushing and folding it, until it is smooth, soft, and easy to mold.

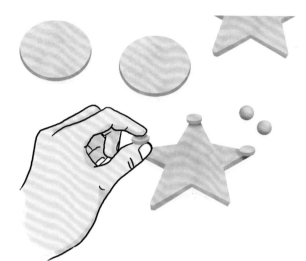

4 Using the cutters, cut out star shapes and small circles. Then take small pieces of dough and make them into balls by rolling them between you palms. Squash them and push them onto the points of the stars.

5 Lay the badges on a baking sheet. Ask an adult to help you put them in an oven at the lowest heat and bake them for about 1½ hours. After this time ask an adult to turn the oven off, but leave the shapes inside to cool completely. This helps to stop the salt dough cracking.

Top tip!

If you want to give your badges and brooches a shiny look paint them with PVA glue.

6 When the pieces have all cooled completely, paint them in bright colors and let them dry.

7 Using the PVA glue, glue the small circles onto the middle of the stars. Glue buttons onto the middle of the circles and let them dry.

YEE Ha!

8 Use PVA glue to stick the brooch pin to the back of the badge. To make certain that it doesn't fall off you could also glue a small scrap of fabric across the back of the pin (see page 123). Let it dry completely before you wear it.

Slate brooch

Slate is a gray rock that splits into smooth layers. You may live in a place where you can pick it up on the beach or in the hills but it is often used for roofing tiles or for decorative covering in the garden and you can find small pieces that way. Find a piece that is thin, light, and has no sharp edges. Wildlife, like hedgehogs or little birds, looks great with the natural color of the slate.

You will need

Small piece of slate

Paint, such as metallic ceramic paint or acrylics

Fine paintbrush

Fine black marker pen

Brooch pin

PVA glue or strong glue (see page 123)

1 Paint a base coat of metallic paint in the shape of a hedgehog, or your chosen design, onto the slate piece. (You may wish to use the template on page 125.)

2 When the metallic paint is dry, paint some white bristles or other decoration on top of the design.

3 With a black marker pen, build up your design by adding some more bristles and an eye and nose.

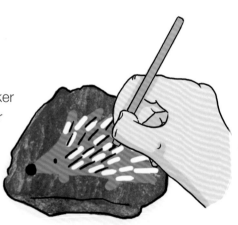

Natural STONE jewelry

(4) Glue the brooch pin onto the back of the slate. Let it dry thoroughly before wearing.

Felt flower brooches

Layer colorful felt flowers together and finish with a button to create funky badges for a favorite jacket.

You will need

Templates on page 125

Paper

Scissors

Pencil

Squares of felt in 3 different colors

Felt glue

Button, about ¾ inch (2 cm) in diameter

Needle

Thread

Metal brooch back

1 Photocopy the flower template and circle on page 125 and cut them out. Place the flower template on the felt and draw around it. Make sure the pencil line shows up clearly. You could pin it to stop the template moving.

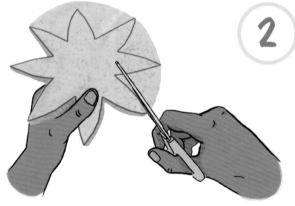

2 Cut out the flower shape carefully with scissors. The easiest way to cut it out is to cut a circle around the flower at the tips of the petals and then cut inward from the circle to the center along the sides of the petals. Cut out another flower and one circle shape for each brooch.

3 Lay one felt flower on the table. Put a dab of glue in the center and lay the other flower on top so that the petals of the bottom flower peep between the petals of the top flower. Put another dab of glue in the center and lay the felt circle on top. Let the glue dry.

4 Place the button right in the middle of the felt circle. Thread the needle and tie a knot in the thread. From the back of the flower stitch up through all three layers of felt and through one of the button holes. Come back down through the other hole. Go up and down through the button four or five times. Finish off at the back by stitching a few small stitches in one place on top of one another. Cut off the thread.

Funky FELT flowers

5 Spread a line of glue along the metal brooch back and stick it in place on the back of the flower, pressing down firmly to finish. Allow the brooch to dry before you wear it.

Twinkling animal brooches

Small children will love these sparkly animal brooches. You could make them for younger brothers and sisters to decorate their toy bags.

You will need

Parchment paper

White air-drying clay

Rolling pin

Animal cookie cutters

Poster paints

Paintbrush

PVA glue

Sparkly diamanté flowers

Brooch pins

1 Cover a work surface with parchment paper. This will protect the surface as well as prevent the clay from sticking. Take a lump of clay from the block and roll it flat with the rolling pin. It needs to be about ¼ inch (5 mm) thick. Don't roll it too thin or the brooches will snap.

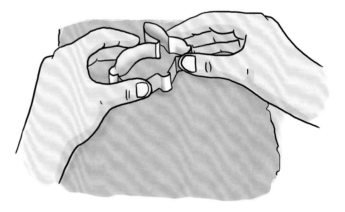

2 Using cookie cutters, cut out some animal shapes. Let the shapes dry. This can take up to 24 hours, but placing the animals somewhere warm will speed up the drying time.

A touch of SPARKLE!

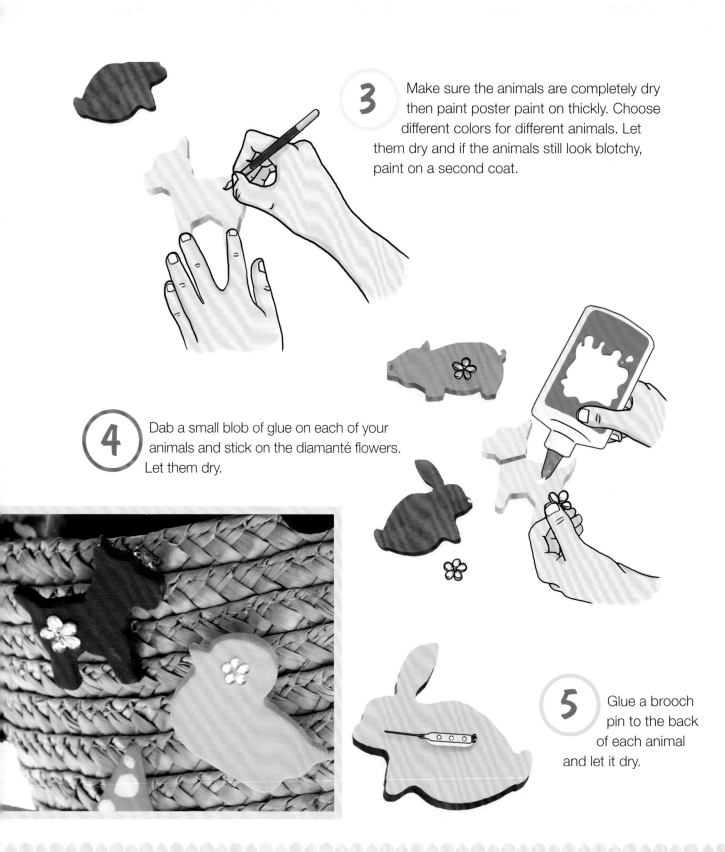

3 Make sure the animals are completely dry then paint poster paint on thickly. Choose different colors for different animals. Let them dry and if the animals still look blotchy, paint on a second coat.

4 Dab a small blob of glue on each of your animals and stick on the diamanté flowers. Let them dry.

5 Glue a brooch pin to the back of each animal and let it dry.

Tissue paper flower brooch

Make these high-impact, big, fun, paper flower corsages from dazzlingly bright tissue paper for a party, or from gentle colors like white, pink, or powder blue to go with a bridesmaid's dress.

You will need

....

1 sheet of tissue paper

Scissors

Pipe cleaner

PVA glue

Brooch pin

Small paper craft flower

1 Tissue paper usually comes folded. Unfold the sheet of tissue paper—there should be a crease down the center—cut it in half lengthwise along this crease. Lay the two halves on top of each other and fold them in half lengthwise again, then cut down the crease so that you have four long strips.

2 Place the four sheets of paper, on top of each other, on a flat work surface with the shortest edge closest to you. Fold the paper up by ¾ inch (2 cm). Press the fold flat. Turn all the sheets over and fold the paper up by the same amount on this side. Press the fold flat and turn back over. Keep going until the end so that your paper is zigzagged all the way up.

Pretty paper FLOWERS

3 Using scissors, cut around both ends of the zigzagged paper to make them petal-shaped.

4 Hold the zigzagged paper firmly and wrap a pipe cleaner around the middle. Try to pull it as tightly as possible so the paper is squeezed up in the middle. Twist the pipe cleaner ends together to hold it firm.

5 Make the flower shape by slowly pulling the sections of tissue paper apart. Do this gently so that you don't rip the paper. When you have fluffed out all the petals to make your flower, cut off the excess pipe cleaner.

Top tip!

Why not make your flower brooch into a bracelet? Pin your flower onto a length of satin ribbon and tie it around your wrist.

6 Use glue to stick the brooch pin to the back of the flower and let it dry. Turn the flower over and glue the paper flower motif in the middle of the flower to finish it off.

Cupcake brooch

Another project for practicing your sewing skills—this eye-catching 3D brooch looks cute on denim jackets and hand-knitted woolly cardigans.

You will need

Templates on page 126

Paper for templates

Scissors

1 sheet of pink felt

1 square of striped fabric

Pencil

Felt glue

Needle

Cotton thread

Crystal seed beads

Large-eyed needle

Embroidery floss (thread)

Batting (wadding)

1 red button

Brooch pin

1 Make a photocopy of the templates on page 126 and carefully cut them out. Place the templates onto the felt and striped fabric and draw around them with a pencil. You will need to cut one frosting shape from pink felt, one cupcake from pink felt, and one cupcake from striped fabric. Cut out the pieces.

2 Using a few dabs of felt glue, stick the frosting onto the striped cupcake. Let it dry for a few minutes.

3 Now sew on crystal seed beads to look like sprinkles. Thread the needle with cotton thread and knot it. Pull the needle through from behind where you want the first bead to be, thread on the bead, and take the needle back through the felt and fabric to make a stitch with a bead inside. Bring it up to the front again where you want the next bead to be and so on. Have the beads scattered across the frosting. When you have sewn them all on, take your needle through to the back and sew a few stitches over and over in one place to secure the thread.

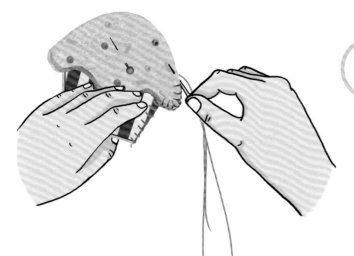

4 Pin the front of the cake (with the frosting) to the felt back of the cake. Thread the large-eyed needle with embroidery floss (thread) and stitch the two sides together using blanket stitch (see page 121). Begin at the right bottom corner and stitch around to the left bottom corner so that the bottom is still unstitched.

5 Leaving your needle threaded and still attached, stuff a little batting (wadding) up into the cupcake to plump it out, then finish sewing up the bottom.

6 Sew the red button at the top of the cake (see page 122), to look like a cherry.

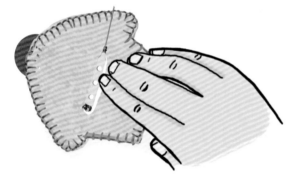

7 Attach the brooch pin to the back, either by stitching it on or by using a dab of glue—depending on the type of pin you are using. If you are using glue, let the glue dry overnight before you wear the brooch.

Mmmmm **CUPCAKE!**

Chapter 4

Hair and Bag Accessories

Fuzzy dinosaur badge 100

Pompom bag charm 102

Sequinned hair band 106

Tassel bag charm 109

Button hair barrette 112

Candy hair clips 114

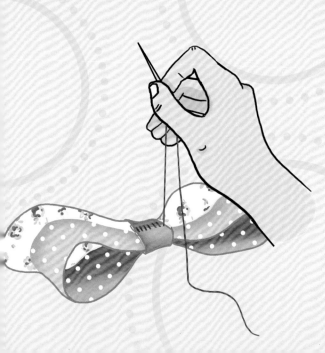

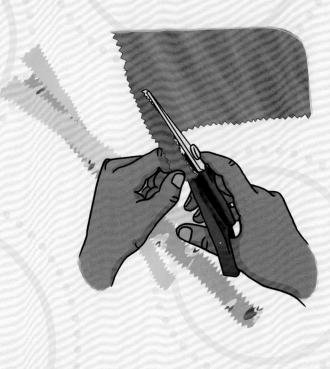

Fuzzy dinosaur badge

Your younger brothers and sisters will love these funny, fuzzy dinosaur badges. Use sturdy card and patterned gift wrap for the bodies. A googly eye and spots of fuzzy felt add to the fun!

You will need

Template on page 126

Glue stick

1 sheet of card (card from a cereal box would do fine)

Patterned gift wrap—small pieces are all you need

Paper for template

Scissors

Pencil

Small scraps of felt in 2 different colors

PVA glue

1 googly eye

Brooch pin

1 Use the glue stick to coat the card in glue. Place your gift wrap on the glued surface, patterned side up, and smooth it down with your hands to make sure there aren't any bubbles or creases. Let it dry for a few minutes.

2 Make a photocopy of the dinosaur template on page 126. Cut it out and place it on top of the gift wrap. Draw around it and cut it out.

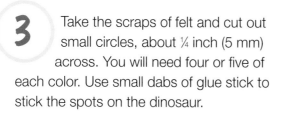

3 Take the scraps of felt and cut out small circles, about ¼ inch (5 mm) across. You will need four or five of each color. Use small dabs of glue stick to stick the spots on the dinosaur.

DOTTY dinosaurs!

4 Put a dab of PVA glue on the head of the dinosaur and stick on the googly eye. Let it dry for a little while before you turn it over to stick on the brooch pin.

5 Glue the brooch pin onto the back of the dinosaur with another dab of PVA glue. Let it dry completely before wearing.

Pompom bag charm

Pompoms are fun to make and this bag charm will guarantee that your plain old school backpack stands out from the crowd, and will make an ordinary bag bright and different.

You will need

Paper for template

Template on page 126

Pencil

Pointed scissors

1 sheet of thick card

Yarn (wool) in at least two colors

Large-eyed needle

Snake or chain key ring

Narrow ribbon

A few big wooden beads

1 Photocopy the pompom template on page 126, cut it out, and cut out the inner circle too. Trace around the template onto the card, twice, with a pencil. Cut out the card circles. With the point of your scissors make a hole in the center of each circle and cut out the inner circles.

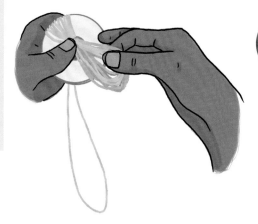

2 Cut a length of yarn (wool) which is about 3 feet (1 m) long. Wind the yarn around your fingers to make it into a loose ball. Put the two card rings together and begin to wrap the long length of yarn around them, pushing the ball of yarn through the middle hole and back around the edge.

3 Keep winding the yarn around the cardboard ring, pulling it quite tightly as you go. Keep going until the whole ring is covered with yarn several layers thick and the hole in the center of the ring is completely full (you may have to use a needle toward the end to push the yarn through the hole). If your yarn runs out halfway through, simply add another length of yarn and keep on wrapping.

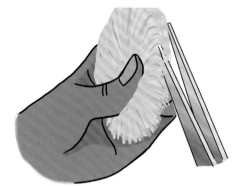

4 Now use scissors to cut around the edge of the woolen ring—push the bottom blade of the scissors down through the yarn between the two cardboard discs and begin snipping the yarn.

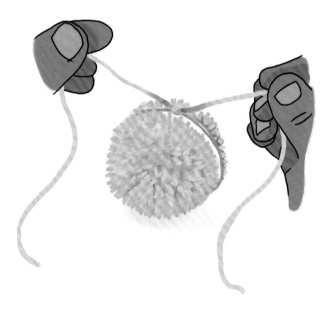

5 When you have snipped all the way round, take another length of yarn about 14 inches (35 cm) long—it can be the same or a different color. Wrap it round the pompom between the two cardboard discs a couple of times, keeping both ends long. Pull it tight and tie it tightly in a double knot. Now tie the long ends together to make a loop for attaching the pompom to the key ring.

Fluffy **POMPOM** *fun!*

6 Carefully peel away the card rings, and fluff up the pompom. If you take the rings off carefully you can use them again for your next pompom. Make two or three pompoms in this way. Make the loops slightly different lengths so they hang at different heights.

7 To hang the pompoms on the key ring, push the end of the loops through the small ring, pass the pompom through the yarn loop, and pull it tight.

8 Add variety to your charm with some wooden beads. Knot a length of narrow ribbon into a loop with a knot large enough so the beads won't pull off. Thread on a couple of wooden beads and attach the ribbon to the key ring in the same way as you did the pompoms.

Sequinned hair band

Make a big beautiful bow to wear in your hair for a special occasion. You could make it in fabrics to match your outfit. If you are lucky enough to have a sewing machine, this is a great project for you. If not, you can stitch it by hand instead.

You will need

2½ x 12 inches (6.5 x 30 cm) each of pink dotted and floral fabrics

3 x 2 inches (7.5 x 5 cm) piece of coral pink cotton

Needle and thread

Pins

Pink sequins and beads

36 inches (90 cm) of pink ribbon

Hair band

PVA glue

1 Put the dotted and floral fabrics together with right sides facing, pin them, and machine stitch along the top and bottom edges. Alternatively, sew them by hand with small neat backstitches (see page 120).

2 Turn right side out and ask an adult to help you press the strip so that the seams run down the middle on each side and you have a band that is half flowery and half dotty.

3 Fold each end up to the center, overlap the ends slightly, and pin in place. Starting with a few stitches over and over in one place to secure the thread, stitch across the band, through all three layers with a row of small running stitches (see page 120). End with a few tiny finishing stitches over and over in one place.

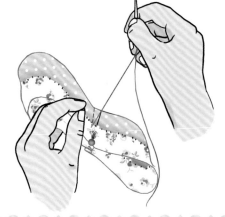

4 Take the piece of coral fabric and ask an adult to help you press each side under by about ¼ inch (5 mm) to hide the raw edges.

A big BEAUTIFUL bow

5 Wrap the coral fabric around the bow so that the bow gathers slightly in the center. At the back turn under the ends so no raw edges show and stitch the ends together using straight stitch (see page 121).

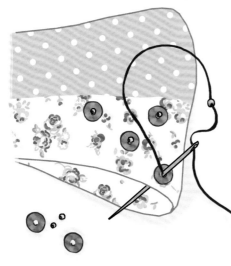

6 Decorate the bow with a few sequins and beads. To stitch on a sequin with a bead, knot the thread and push the needle up through the fabric from the inside of the bow (so the knot doesn't show), then thread on the sequin and tiny bead, take the thread over the bead and back down through the hole in the sequin. Sew on several sequins and beads scattered over one half of the bow, then finish off as before. Sew more sequins and beads on the other half.

7 To cover the hair band, first spread a little PVA glue on the end of the ribbon and glue it to the inside of the hair band. Let it dry. Now carefully wind the ribbon around the hair band, being sure not to leave any spaces where the plastic shows through. When you have finished, cut off the ribbon so that the end is inside the hair band and glue it down. Let it dry.

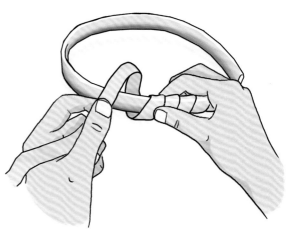

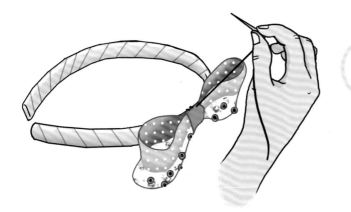

8 Finally, stick the bow to the hair band and let it dry. To make sure that it is secure you could put a stitch in the back of the bow, take the thread under the hair band, and stitch into the bow again. Do this a few times and end with some finishing stitches.

Tassel bag charm

This is a fun accessory that you can make using scraps of fabric. Try mixing bold patterns and solid-colored fabric together and add some colorful beads to really make it stand out.

You will need

- 4 pieces of assorted cotton fabric
- Pinking shears
- Piece of thin cord
- Sticky tape
- 2 big wooden beads
- Metal jump ring
- Bag charm attachment

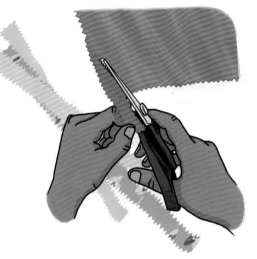

1 Take the first fabric and use pinking shears to cut a strip that is 10 inches (25 cm) long and ¾ inch (2 cm) wide. Cut two more strips like this from two different fabrics. Finally, cut a longer strip from the fourth fabric, this time about 16 inches (40 cm) long and ¾ inch (2 cm) wide.

2 Lie the fabric strips on top of each other flat on the table. Find the middle and use the longer strip to tie all the strips together.

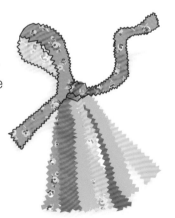

3 Hold the strips in the center so they dangle down double. Take one half of the longer strip and make it into a long loop (making sure it is long enough for the two beads to thread onto).

Add **CHARM** to your bag with trendy **TASSELS!**

4 Wrap the other half of the strip around the bottom of the loop to hold it in place and tie the two ends together. Trim off the excess fabric.

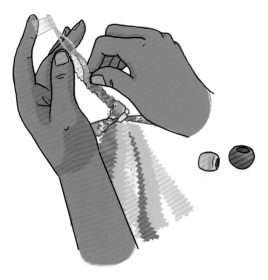

5 Thread a short length of thin cord through the loop of fabric and tape the ends together with a little sticky tape. Now you can push this stiffened end easily through the two wooden beads and pull them down over the thicker fabric loop. Cut off the cord.

6 Take the jump ring and thread it through the fabric loop at the top of the beads. Loop the bag charm attachment onto the jump ring and close the ring as tightly as possible.

Button hair barrette

Jazz up a plain barrette (hair slide) by adding felt and bright buttons. See what buttons you have around the house, take them from old clothes, or even hunt for them in your local thrift (charity) store.

You will need

Plain hair barrette (hair slide)

Glue stick

Colored felt

Scissors

Assorted plastic buttons

PVA glue

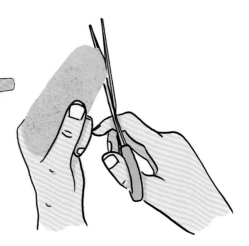

1 Roughly cut out a piece of felt that is bigger all around than the barrette.

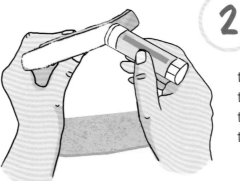

2 Hold the underside of the barrette in one hand and use the other hand to spread glue on the flat surface of the barrette with the glue stick. You will need quite a thick layer. Be sure to spread it right to the edges.

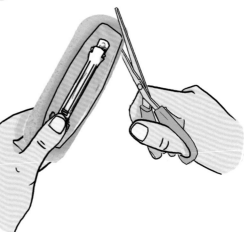

3 Press the felt onto the glued surface of the barrette and let it dry. When dry, use sharp scissors to cut neatly around the barrette shape.

Bright as a BUTTON!

4 Choose enough buttons to fit all along the barrette. Decide which order you would like them to be in and arrange them in a line on the work surface. Starting from one end, apply a dab of PVA glue to the felt surface and stick on the first button. Continue to apply glue and buttons along the length of the barrette. Let it dry completely before wearing.

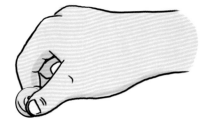

Candy hair clips

Make these eye-catching hair clips from modeling clay—it's so easy to use. Put together some delicious looking licorice candies—stick them to a hair clip and you're ready for the party! What's more, it's easier to make several beads than just one so make plenty and give them to your friends.

You will need

Parchment paper

Modeling clay (such as Fimo) in black, purple, turquoise, yellow, and white

Modeling tool or a round-bladed knife

Baking sheet lined with parchment paper

Colorful metal hair clips

PVA glue

1 To make the square candies, first lay a sheet of parchment paper on your work surface to protect it. Take a new block of clay (it's better to work straight from the block so that you always get a nice clean edge) and your modeling tool or knife and carefully cut a slice of clay about ⅛ inch (3 mm) thick. Cut several slices of white and black and one of each bright color.

2 Sandwich three, four, or five slices together, alternating the bright colors with the black and white. Press them down gently so that the slices stick to each other.

Eye-catching HAIR CLIPS!

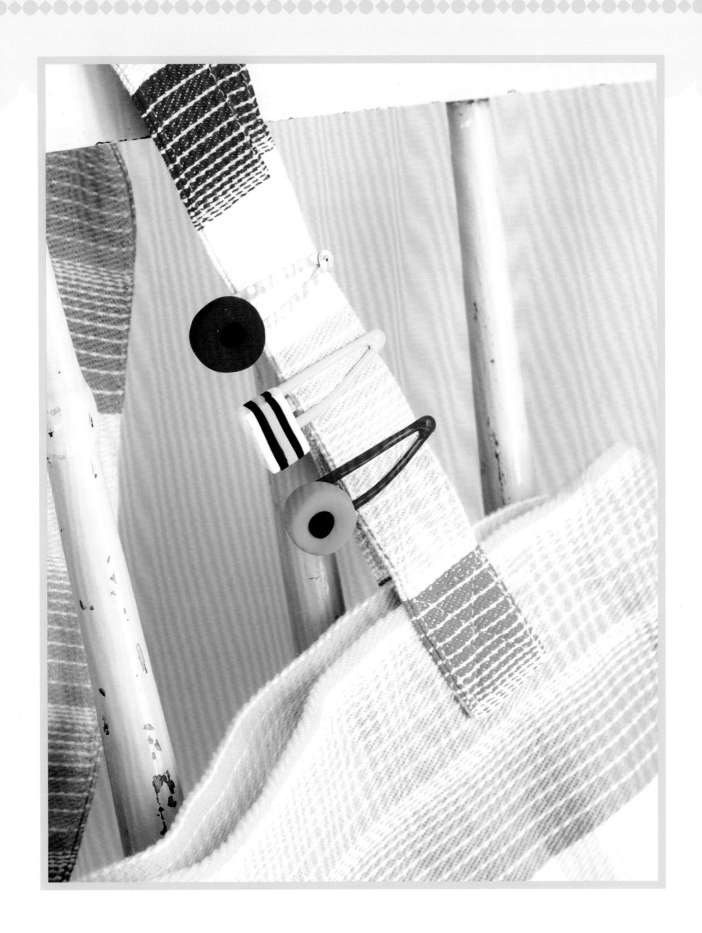

3 Take a stack of clay slices, and trim off each end so that the candy becomes a square shape and the edges are lined up neatly. Place them on the lined baking sheet.

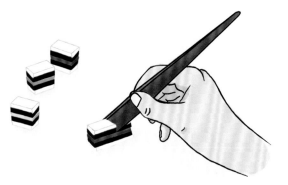

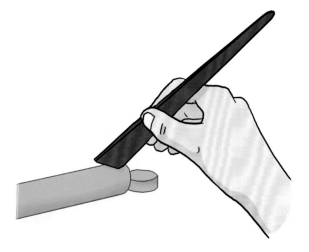

4 To make the round candy, roll a sausage of colored clay, about 1 inch (2.5 cm) thick. Use your modeling tool or knife to cut off the end of the sausage so you have a nice flat surface to begin, and then cut it into slices, about ½ inch (1 cm) thick.

5 Place a slice on the work surface, place the wrong end of a pencil in the center, and press gently, so that the slice is slightly pushed in to make a dip.

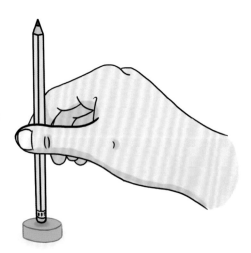

6 Take a small piece of black clay and roll it into a ball. Place the ball into the dip and press it down lightly until it sticks and has flattened out. It will look as though the colored clay is wrapped around the black clay.

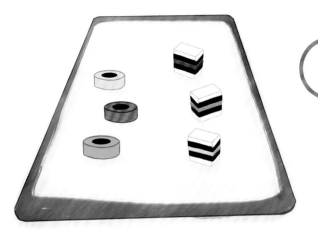

7 Place the round beads with the square ones on the lined baking sheet and ask an adult to help you bake them in the oven, following the instructions on the packet of clay.

8 When the beads are cool, stick them to the ends of the hair clips using PVA glue. Allow the glue to dry overnight before you wear them.

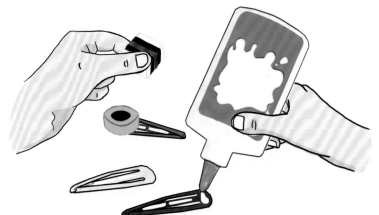

Your jewelry crafting box

As you will see from the projects in this book, jewelry can be made from all sorts of different materials, from fabric and felt, to salt dough, recycled cardboard tubes, and even found objects like shells and stones!

For all the projects, you will need some craft materials and basic equipment. We suggest you gather together the following:

* Pencil

* Ruler

* Tape measure

* Plain paper

* Squared paper

* Thin card

* Scissors for cutting paper

* Sharp scissors for cutting fabric

* Pins

* Needles, including some big ones with big eyes

* Pinking shears (if you have them)

* PVA glue, felt glue, and glue sticks

* Paints and paintbrushes

* Fine felt-tipped pens

It is also a good idea to start a collection of fabrics and other materials, so look out for the following:

* Pretty patterned fabrics—remnants or worn out clothes

* Squares of felt in different colors

* Ribbons and braids—look out for ones used to wrap gifts or chocolates

* Beads in an assortment of colors and sizes

* Cotton thread, embroidery floss (thread), and yarn (wool) in different colors

* Raffia string, thick thread for threading, beading elastic or thread

* Buttons—especially pretty ones. Cut them off clothes that are too worn out to go to the thrift (charity) store)

* Colored tissue paper and scraps of gift wrap

Quite a few of the projects require brooch, bracelet, or necklace fastenings. These are not expensive and it would be a good idea to buy a selection of these.

Remember to wear an apron when you work with paint or glue and to cover work surfaces with some old newspaper.

Techniques

Most of the projects in this book are so simple that they can be made without any special techniques—threading beads, tying knots, and gluing are all you need to know for some of them. However, there are a few techniques that will come in very useful—perhaps you know some of these already? If not, follow the instructions below.

Sewing techniques

Using templates

A few of the projects in this book have templates—these will help you to recreate the projects exactly as they appear in the book. To use them:

1 Either photocopy the template for your project from the back of the book or trace it onto thin paper. Cut out the shape to make a pattern.

2 Pin this pattern onto your fabric, making sure that the fabric is flat with no creases. If the template is too small to pin, hold the template in place with your thumb and forefinger. Draw round the template in pencil, making sure that the pencil line shows up clearly.

3 Carefully cut it out with scissors, following the pencil lines. Remove the pins and you're ready to go!

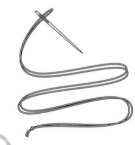

Threading a needle
You won't be able to start sewing without threading your needle!

1 Thread your needle with about 25 inches (65 cm) of thread or yarn (wool). Pull about 6 inches (15 cm) of the thread through the needle. Tie two knots on top of each other at the other end.

2 For a double thread, which is stronger, pull the thread through the needle until the thread is doubled over and tie a knot in the two ends together.

Running stitch

This is the simplest stitch and can be used in embroidery and for joining two layers of fabric together. It is very easy to do, but not very strong.

Secure the end of the thread with a few small stitches. Push the needle down through the fabric a little way along, then bring it back up through the fabric a little further along. Repeat to form a row of stitches.

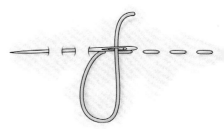

Finishing stitching

It is important to finish off all your stitching, so that it doesn't come undone.

When you have finished stitching, sew a few tiny stitches over and over in the same place on the back of the fabric. Then trim off your thread.

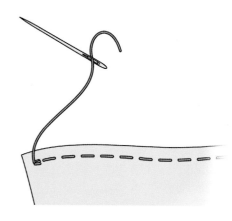

Backstitch

This is a very useful stitch, since it is strong and similar to the stitches used on a sewing machine. It makes a solid line of stitches.

1 Start as if you were sewing running stitch. Sew one stitch and bring the needle back up to start the second stitch.

2 This time, instead of going forward, go back and push the needle through at the end of your first stitch.

3 Bring it out again a stitch length past the thread. Keep going to make an even line of stitches with no gaps.

Straight stitch

Straight stitch is used to sew one shape to another. You can also use individual straight stitches to create decorative stitches, or sew a series of them to create simple patterns.

Pass the needle through to the front, pulling the thread completely through the fabric, and then take it through to the back again. Repeat to make as many stitches as needed, making sure they are all the same length.

Blanket stitch

This makes a pretty edge when you are sewing two layers of felt or fabric together.

1 Bring the needle through at the edge of the fabric.

2 Push the needle back through the fabric a short distance from the edge and loop the thread under the needle. Pull the needle and thread as far as you can to make the first stitch.

3 Make another stitch to the right of this and again loop the thread under the needle. Continue along the fabric and finish with a few small stitches or a knot on the underside.

Stars

You can make star shapes using straight stitch (see above).

Sew four overlapping straight stitches to create a star shape. Start by sewing a cross of two stitches, then add the other two to complete the eight-pointed star.

Sewing on buttons

You can use buttons as decorations—and you never know when you'll need to sew a button on some clothes!

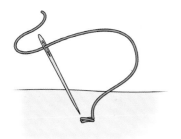

1 Mark the place where you want the button to go. Push the needle up from the back of the fabric and sew a few stitches over and over in this place.

2 Now bring the needle up through one of the holes in the button. Push the needle back down through the second hole and through the fabric. Bring it back up through the first hole. Repeat this five or six times. If there are four holes in the button, use all four of them to make a cross pattern. Make sure that you keep the stitches close together under the middle of the button.

3 Finish with a few small stitches over and over on the back of the fabric and trim the thread.

Other techniques
Reef knot

This is a strong knot to tie two pieces of string together or to tie two ends together to make a loop.

1 Take the left end of the string, pass it across the right end, and twist it underneath.

2 The ends have now swapped places. Take what has now become the right end and pass it over the left end, twist it underneath, and bring it up through the loop you have just made.

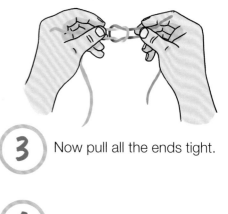

3 Now pull all the ends tight.

4 This little rhyme will help you remember: "Left over right and under, right over left and under."

Braiding (plaiting)

Braiding makes a stronger length of yarn or string and is also used to create a pretty decorative effect.

1 Knot three equal pieces of twine or yarn (wool) together at one end. Hold the knotted end firm with a bulldog clip, stick it down with some tack, or put a heavy book on top (or ask someone to hold it for you).

2 Take the right strand over the middle strand—this then becomes the middle strand.

3 Take the left strand over the middle strand—this then becomes the middle strand.

4 Keep repeating right over middle, left over middle, until you reach the end. Tie the strands together in a knot.

Using glue

There are lots of different types of glue available but you will only really need two types for the projects in this book. PVA glue is very versatile and will stick lots of different materials together. It is non-toxic and easy to use and the good thing about it is that it dries clear so it doesn't matter if you use too much. Glue sticks are good for sticking paper but are not so good for heavier items. Felt glue is a non-toxic glue that is ideal for sticking pieces of felt together and is used for some of the projects in this book.

If you are making a brooch or corsage you will probably need to fix a brooch finding to the back—these can be fixed using PVA glue. To use a safety pin instead of a brooch clasp, cut a small rectangle of fabric, apply PVA glue to one side, and then place it over the fixed bar of the pin.

Some of the projects in this book may require a slightly stronger glue—for example, the Slate brooch (see page 84). Strong glue can be toxic and should be used with great care so always ask an adult to help you.

Templates

All the templates provided here are at full size, so can be photocopied or traced as they are. See page 119 for more detail on how to use templates.

Shell pendant, page 24

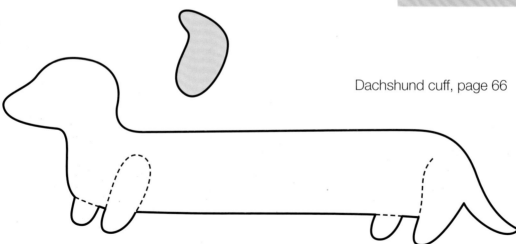

Dachshund cuff, page 66